Know About What Amazing & Interesting Fun Facts That Everyone Should Know

By Bandana Ojha

All rights reserved. This book or any portion thereof may not be reproduced or used in any manner without the express written permission of the author.

Copyright © 2022By the author.

Introduction

Filled with up-to-date information, fascinating & fun facts this book "Know About Whales: 100+ Amazing & Interesting Fun Facts" is the best book for kids to find out more about the amazing creature Whale. This book would satisfy the children's curiosity and help them to understand why whales are special—and what makes them different from other animals. The book gives a story, history, detailed science, explores the interesting facts about largest blue whales, killer whale, sperm whale, fin whale, gray whale, bowhead whale, humpback whale in the ocean world. This is a great chance for every kid to expand their knowledge about whales and impress family and friends with all discovered and never knew before fun facts.

1. Blue whale is the largest animal on the planet. It can be found in all oceans of the world. They usually spend the summer in arctic water and migrate to southern waters during wintertime.

2. Another name for whales is cetacea, which is from the Greek word Keto, who was the goddess of sea monsters.

3. The Blue Whales are said to have evolved from hippopotamuses. Whales developed streamlined shape responsible for graceful movement into the water.

4. Whales are mammals that have adapted to a life in the ocean, but their ancestors lived on land. Whales return to the ocean about 53 – 54 million years ago

5. Some of the locations blue whales can be found living in include Antarctica, the North Atlantic and North Pacific Oceans and the Indian Ocean.

6. In the context of a group or family male whales are often referred to as bulls, females are called cows and babies are commonly known as calves.

7. When it comes to lifespan the average lifespan of a whale can range from 20 – 200 years depending on the whales' species, overall health, social life, and environment.

8. Blue whales are the fastest growing animal or plant on Earth.

9. When fully grown this massive marine mammal can reach lengths more than 100 ft. and weight more than 150 tons.

10. The blue whale's heart is huge as in the size of a car, its beat can be detected from two miles away.

11. A blue whale's tongue alone weighs as much as an elephant.

12. Blue whales are the loudest animals on the planet. The call of a blue whale reaches 188 decibels. Their language of

pulses, groans, and moans can be heard by others up to 1,000 miles.

13. Whales swim to where Krill are present in huge numbers and just swallow them along with water. The water is spat out with tongue while the krill is stuck in the bristles. Once the water is completely removed, Whales swallow the prey wholly.

14. Despite being such a huge animal the blue whale can only consume small prey since its esophagus is too small to consume larger sources of food and it is

unable to chew its food and break it down into smaller pieces.

15. Blue Whales do not possess teeth. Their jaws are powerful and contain bristles.

16. Blue Whales do not possess gills. It means they cannot extract oxygen from water to breath. A blowhole is located on top of their head and is used for sucking in large amounts of air when it swims to the surface.

17. Blowhole functions like nostrils. Blue Whales have two blowholes located on the left and right side of the head. So, it is pretty much like humans who breathe through one nostril for most of the time.

18. Blue whales are solitary creatures. Unlike other baleen whales, blue whales travel either by solo or in pairs, rather than in groups.

19. They communicate to one another by using loud low-pitched moans and whines which can be heard many miles away.

20. When they dive back under the water the color of the water and the light from the sun make these marine mammals look a deeper blue than they really are.

21. They travel a lot, spending summers feeding in polar regions and making the long trip to the Equator as winter comes along. While they have a cruising speed of 5 MPH, they can accelerate up to 20 MPH when needed.

22. The most concentrated Blue Whale habitats in winter are the waters off Baja California, Mexico and Pico Island, Portugal. During the summer, they frequent Quebec's Gulf of St. Lawrence and Husavik, Iceland. Chile, the Maldives, and Sri Lanka.

23. Because the blue whale can travel through the ocean without worrying about being hunted themselves, they are known as apex predators, which means they are predators that do not have any predators of their own.

23. During their migration trips the blue whale can travel thousands of miles from one location to the next.

24. The excessive amounts of food they consume during feeding season helps these marine mammals build up their supply of blubber which they will rely on for energy during their long trip.

25. The blue whale has a very small triangular dorsal fin as compared to the larger dorsal fin of many other whale species and the flippers which are used for steering are relatively short when compared to the rest of its body.

26. While they migrate, most whales will forgo eating food and live primarily off blubber/body fat and stored calories.

27. To minimize their energy expenditure and limit the number of calories they use these marine mammals travel an average of 3 – 6 miles per hour during their migration, however when they feel threatened or agitated, they can reach speeds of over 30 miles per hour for short bursts.

28. The average gestation period for a female blue whale usually lasts 10 – 12 months.

29. At the end of the gestation term the female will give birth to a single offspring.

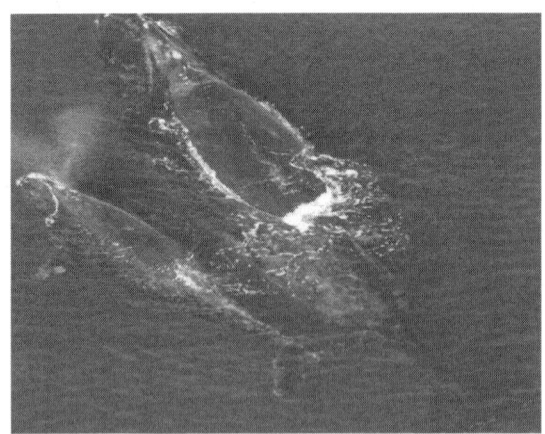

30. The baby blue whale can measure in 20 – 25 ft. long when born (1/4 – 1/3 the size of an adult blue whale).

31. For the first 6 – 9 months the newborn will be fed milk from its mother nipple.

32. The milk is full of fat and nutrients that will the child develop during its first months of life.

33. Some baby whales may also use their mouth/tongue as a seal to help prevent the milk from traveling through

the water to ensure that they are receiving important food and nutrients.

34. After the child stops being nursed by its mother it will begin to start consuming solid foods and hunting for its own prey.

35. As with other baleen whale species when the blue whale reaches adult hood the female whales typically grow to be larger than their male counterparts.

36. Killer whales are highly social and often travel in groups that are matrifocal—a family unit focused or centered on the mother.

37. Blue whale's age is most reliably measured using ear plugs.

38. The estimated lifespan of a blue whale is 70 – 90 years, they are also

one of the oldest living marine mammals.

39. The oldest recorded blue whale was estimated to have a lifespan of 110 years.

40. Whales need to sleep – but they only put one side of their brain to sleep at a time, like birds do

41. Gray whales make one of the longest annual migrations of any mammal: they travel about 10,000 miles (16,000 km) round trip.

42. Their lungs are adapted for diving – trachea extends all the way to the center of their lungs – our cartilaginous windpipe only extends as far as the branching

43. All whales have multi-chambered stomachs, inherited from their ungulate ancestors, but of no use in the ocean, including blue whales. Baleen whale stomachs have 3 chambers – forestomach (often contains rocks, to help the muscular walls grind up fish bones and crustacean exoskeletons), main stomach, and pyloric stomach.

44. The longest living whale is the Bowhead whale. They can live over 200 years, making them the oldest living mammals on earth.

45. Sperm whales are the loudest animals on Earth. Their calls reach up to 230 decibels.

46. Scientists have noticed that humpback whales around the world have been rescuing animals being hunted by orcas.

47. Despite being called killer whales; orcas belong to the dolphin family Delphinidae. They're the only species in their genus, but their closest relatives are dolphin species

48. So orcas are dolphins not whales.

49. The Latin name for orca or killer whale is Orcinus orca. Orcinus translates to "of the kingdom of the dead" and is probably derived from Roman God of the underworld Orcus, a reference to the fierce hunting reputation of this animal.

50. A Cuvier's beaked whale has been recorded to dive to a depth of 3km for over 2 hours.

51. Beluga whales have flexible necks, allowing them to move their heads. Their complex communication

repertoire of whistles, clicks, and chirps has prompted the nickname "canaries of the sea."

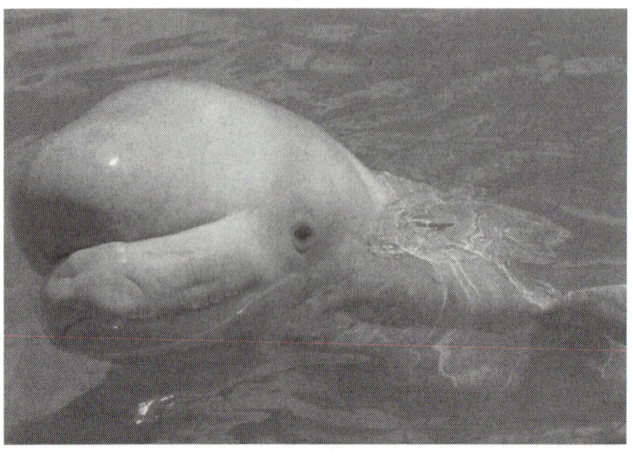

52. Sperm whales were almost driven to extinction by commercial whalers who sought the whales' blubber and the unique oil derived from the "spermaceti organ" found in their massive heads. The spermaceti organ is a key part of their echolocation system with ships.

53. The minke whale is the smallest baleen whale in North American waters.

54. Sperm whales are also champion divers. Adults can stay underwater for almost two hours and dive to depths of 2,000 meters, maybe more.

55. The sperm whale's huge head, which is up to a third of its overall body length, houses the heaviest brain in the animal kingdom - up to 9kg. The head also consists of a cavity large enough to park a car inside that contains a yellowish wax called spermaceti.

56. The bowhead whale, which lives exclusively in the Arctic, has the thickest blubber of all cetaceans. It can reach a whopping 70cm in thickness.

57. The male narwhal has two teeth. The left one pierces the animal's lip and grows to an incredible 2-3 meters.

58. The blue whales esophagus is so small that it would not be able to swallow an adult human.

59. An individual fin whale pees about 970 liters per day.

60. Sperm whales make the loudest sounds. They have been recorded making a noise at 230 decibels.

61. Blue whales are also very loud. Their call reaches levels up to 188 decibels and can be heard hundreds of miles away. A jet in comparison reaches only 140 decibels. Sounds over 120-130 decibels are painful to human ears.

62. Blue whales are seasonal feeders. They can go up to 6 months without eating when they migrate for breeding.

63. Compared to other body parts, the brain of blue whales is small and weighs only 6.92 kilograms, that's 0.007 percent of its body weight.

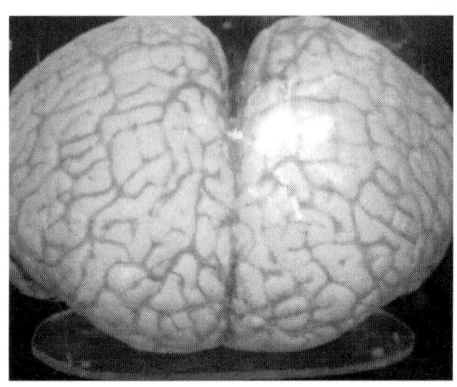

64. Blue whales can consume 500 kilograms of krill in a single mouthful and get half a million calories from it. That is 200 times of what they spend in the act.

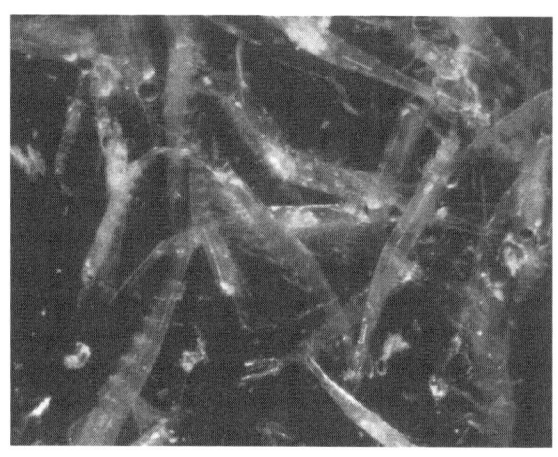

65. Male humpback whales sing the most complex songs and have long, varied, eerie, and beautiful songs that include recognizable sequences of squeaks, grunts, and other sounds.

66. The songs have the largest range of frequencies used by whales, ranging from 20-9,000 Hertz. Only males have been recorded singing.

67. They sing the complex songs only in warm waters, perhaps used for mating purposes. In cold waters, they make rougher sounds, scrapes and

groans, perhaps used for locating large masses of krill.

68. Whales do not drink seawater; instead, they extract water from their food by metabolizing fat.

69. Blue whales sleep while swimming. They use only half of their brain while sleeping.

70. Blue Whales look mottled gray over the surface. When underwater they appear solidly blue. Microorganisms live in the skin of their bellies. It gives a yellowish coloration to the belly.

71. The humpback whale breaches more often than any other whale, sometimes leaving the water completely during a leap. This is quite a feat considering that a humpback whale can weigh as much as 30 tons.

72. Most species of toothed whales live in matrilineal pods, dominated by mothers, aunts, daughters, and sisters. Males typically stay with a pod for only a year or two after birth and then leave to visit other female pods to mate.

73. In about 40 years, a gray whale migrates a total distance that is equivalent to the moon and back.

74. Because whales typically use hearing as their primary sense, they have small eyes in proportion to their overall body size.

75. Blue whales have fairer skin than other types of whales and, consequently, get sunburned more often when they come to the surface to breath, feed their young, and socialize.

76. Scientists believe that the hole in the ozone layer is increasing the number and severity of the burns.

77. Study found that sperm whales sleep in vertical postures just under the surface in passive shallow 'drift-dives', generally during the day.

78. The largest whale in the world was the blue whale at 30 meters and over 180 tons, whereas the smallest was the pygmy sperm whale at 3.5m

79. Because whales have so much blubber, they would easily float. To counteract this, their bones are extra heavy.

80. The beluga whale is the only member of the cetacean order capable of facial expressions.

81. A whale's earwax reveals a whale's age, like the way tree rings reveal the age of tree.

82. Whales are considered one of the most intelligent animals on earth.

83. Not only do they show intellectual abilities, but they also show deep emotions in their ability to connect with others, morn death and celebrate vitality.

84. The sperm whale has the biggest brain on land or in the water, at roughly 16 pounds. However, most of it is filled with fatty, yellow tissue called "junk."

85. When a blue whale exhales, the water from its blowhole can reach almost 30 feet into the air.

86. Baleen whales (in contrast to toothed whales) are also known as "Mysticeti," which is "mustached

whales." While baleen whales have teeth as a fetus, they only develop baleen, which is made of keratin. Baleen is like the ridges on top of a human's mouth.

87. Sperm whales can dive as deep as two miles into the water, and their bodies have unique physiological adaptations to allow them to survive the intense cold and crushing pressure of these dives. They can limit circulation to the brain and other organs, slow the heart to 10 beats per minute to conserve

oxygen, and collapse the lungs and rib cage to withstand pressure.

88. When a blue whale dives into the water, its head is already deeper than most scuba divers dare to go before its tail leaves the surface of the water.

89. Baleen whales use sounds as communication, toothed whales use sound for hunting and navigating.

90. Studies of certain whale pods have shown that whales can develop a social hierarchy, play games together, teach each other survival strategies and hunt in cohesive well-organized groups.

91. During the 20th century, whalers killed nearly 3 million whales, and nearly wiped out 90% of all blue whales.

92. Humpback and blue whales remain close to extinction.

93. Baleen whales make low frequency sounds; toothed whales make high-frequency sounds.

94. The North Atlantic right whale is one of the most endangered whales. Only around 400-500 individuals survive, living along the east coast of North America.

95. A few hundred right whales also live in the North Pacific while the

Western Pacific gray whale may be down to the last 150 whales.

96. Number of blue whales decreased drastically in the first half of the 20th century when whalers hunted them nearly to extinction.

97. 18th and 19th century whalers hunted whales for their oil, which was used as lamp fuel and lubricant.

98. Today, blue whales are under protection and their number managed to increase a bit. They are still endangered animals with less than 4500 animals left on the planet.

99. The most endangered species of whale is Bryde's whale. There are only about 50 living in the Gulf of Mexico.

100. Besides hunting, blue whales are threatened by ocean pollution,

increased sea traffic (they die after collisions with boats), climate changes and oil spills.

101. Blue whales were hunted in great numbers from then on, reducing their numbers from 350,000 to 1 or 2 thousand.

102. The North Atlantic and North Pacific right whales are among the most endangered of all whales. Only around 400-500 individuals currently exist with fewer than 100 North Pacific right whales remaining.

103. A whale's acoustic bubble used to be about 1000 km, and now it is just 100km.

104. The Western Pacific gray whale may be down to the last 150 individuals.

105. Blue Whale protection comes from two wildlife conservation organizations, such as Whale and Dolphin Conservation, Save the Whales and Sea Shepherd Conservation Society. These NGOs make efforts to prevent whaling, safeguard blue whale

habitats, reconfigure problematic shipping routes, and keep the ocean clean.

106. One of the best ways that a person can help in their own home to save whales is to recycle as much plastic as possible that might otherwise end up in the ocean.

Our other best-selling books for kids are-
Know about **Sharks**: Interesting & Amazing Facts That Everyone Should Know
Know About **Whales**: Interesting & Amazing Facts That Everyone Should Know
Know About **Dinosaurs**: Interesting & Amazing Facts That Everyone Should Know
Know About **Kangaroos**: Interesting & Amazing Facts That Everyone Should Know
Know About **Penguins**: Interesting & Amazing Facts That Everyone Should Know
Know About **Dolphins** :100 Interesting & Amazing Facts That Everyone Should Know
Know About **Elephant:** Interesting & Amazing Facts That Everyone Should Know
All About **New York**: Interesting & Amazing Facts That Everyone Should Know
All About **New Jersey**: Interesting & Amazing Facts That Everyone Should Know
All About **Washington**: Interesting & Amazing Facts That Everyone Should Know
All About **Massachusetts**: 100+ Amazing Facts with Pictures
All About **Florida**: Interesting & Amazing Facts That Everyone Should Know
All About **California**: Interesting & Amazing Facts That Everyone Should Know

All About **Arizona**: Interesting & Amazing Facts That Everyone Should Know
All About **Texas**: Interesting & Amazing Facts That Everyone Should Know
All About **Minnesota**: Interesting & Amazing Facts That Everyone Should Know
All About **Illinois**: Interesting & Amazing Facts That Everyone Should Know
All About **New Mexico**: Interesting & Amazing Facts That Everyone Should Know
All About **Canada**: Interesting & Amazing Facts That Everyone Should Know
All About **Australia**: Interesting & Amazing Facts That Everyone Should Know
All About **Italy**: Interesting & Amazing Facts That Everyone Should Know
All About **France**: Interesting & Amazing Facts That Everyone Should Know
All About **Japan:** Interesting & Amazing Facts That Everyone Should Know
100 Amazing **Quiz Q & A About Penguin**: Never Known Before Penguin Facts
Most Popular **Animal Quiz** book for Kids: 100 amazing animal facts
Quiz Book for Kids: Science, History, Geography, Biology, Computer & Information Technology

English **Grammar** for Kids: Most Easy Way to learn English Grammar

Solar System & Space Science- Quiz for Kids: What You Know About Solar System

English **Grammar Practice** Book for elementary kids: 1000+ Practice Questions with Answers

A to Z of **English Tense**